C is for Cerebral Palsy

A Child's View

Published by Gotcha Apps, LLC
1904 ½ Williams St.
Valdosta, GA 31602

This book provides general information on cerebral palsy. It should not be relied upon as recommending or promoting any specific diagnosis or method of treatment. It is not intended as a substitute for medical advice or for direct diagnosis and treatment of cerebral palsy by a qualified physician. Readers who have questions about cerebral palsy or its treatment should consult with a physician or other qualified health care professional.

ISBN-13: 978-0-9981567-4-3

Cover art and interior artwork by Ikos Ronzkie

Edited by Christy Koury

Text by Amy E. Sturkey, PT

To my mother
who celebrated every step of my life
and taught me all about Love.
I am a physical therapist
today because of you.
Thank you, Mom!

Introduction

Does your child have a friend, family member, or classmate who has cerebral palsy? Would you like your child or the children in your classroom to understand more about cerebral palsy? Are you looking for an engaging way to start a dialogue about cerebral palsy? I wrote this book to solve these challenges.

C is for Cerebral Palsy is a children's picture book in an ABC format. With delightful illustrations, this book teaches typical conditions that a person with cerebral palsy might have. The book uses child-friendly language and is narrated by a 6-year-old with cerebral palsy. *C is for Cerebral Palsy* provides an entertaining way to start a simple educational discussion about cerebral palsy.

I invite you to read this story interactively with your child. Encourage discussions of how you or your friends might be like the child in this book. You might compare and contrast how the child in this book is similar or different from a person you know with cerebral palsy.

I intentionally chose the main character in this story to have more significant limitations and accompanying factors in order to allow a more inclusive discussion of cerebral palsy. You or your child's friends may have more options for movement than the child depicted in this story. There are many people with cerebral palsy with less physical involvement than the child described here.

I believe knowledge helps break down barriers and encourages kindness and patience. Helping children understand cerebral palsy at a young age is powerful. Reading this book will change the life of your child and the lives of people with cerebral palsy that your child meets now and in the future.

C is for Cerebral Palsy

A Child's View

written by:
Amy E. Sturkey, PT

illustrated by:
Ikos Ronzkie

A is for who I Am.
I am a good kid. I am a great friend. I am a big soccer
fan. I love my little sister. I also have cerebral palsy.
I'll tell you about my life with cerebral palsy.

B is for Brain.

The brain is the boss of your body. It controls the way you think, feel and move. It is in the center of your head, right between your ears. I was born too early. That made it easy for my brain to get hurt. Mommy said that before I was born that my brain got a boo-boo. Now the part of my brain that tells my body how to move doesn't work right.

C is for Cerebral Palsy.

I have cerebral palsy. People with cerebral palsy have a hurt spot in their brain that happened around the time they were born. The hurt spot makes some people with cerebral palsy have muscles that are too stiff and tight. Others have muscles that are floppy or jerky. My cerebral palsy makes my arms and legs stiff. My neck and back are weak.

D is for Drinking.

I have trouble drinking and eating. It's hard for me to chew and swallow food. Sometimes I drool. I need someone to mash up my food and help me eat, but I eat all the same foods you do. Chocolate is my favorite. Is it your favorite too?

E is for Eyes.
My eyes don't see that well.
Glasses can't help me see better.
The hurt spot on my brain makes
it hard for me to see.

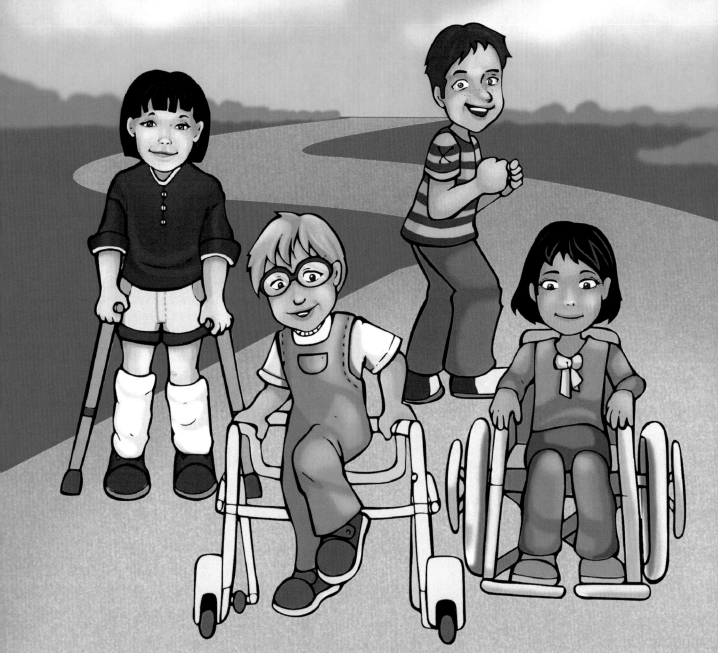

F is for Friends.
I have lots of friends. Some of them have cerebral palsy and can walk with crutches. Some can walk with a walker. Some of my friends can walk by themselves. Since my legs can't walk, my wheelchair helps me move without someone having to carry me.

G is for Go.
I love to go in my wheelchair.
Sometimes, my mommy pushes
me when she runs races. I love
to feel the wind on my face.
I can go, go, go!

H is for Head.
I work hard just to hold up my head. I need help to sit, stand and walk. It's all because of that boo-boo on my brain. My parents and my physical therapist are helping me get stronger.

I is for Intelligence.
Some people with cerebral palsy have trouble learning
and thinking. Some people with cerebral palsy learn
and think just like you. Does intelligence really matter
when we are laughing and having fun together? Come
and talk to me. We can learn a lot from each other.

J is for Joy.
I find joy in lots of things. I love laughing,
cuddling and swinging. I want to be right in the
middle of all the fun. I bet you do too.

K is for Knowing that I am Mommy and Daddy's unexpected gift.
That's what they say! Daddy says I am small, but I am a big teacher. Mommy says I teach people how to slow down and enjoy the moment. I learn and get stronger slowly. My parents celebrate whenever I learn anything new.

L is for my Life.
I will have cerebral palsy my whole life. There are
therapies, medicine, and surgeries that might help me,
but there is no cure, no way to fix my brain...YET.
I am hoping that in my lifetime, that the smart doctors
and scientists are going to help me. Either way,
I know amazing things will happen in my life.

M is for Moving.
I watch all my friends move and play, and I get so
frustrated. I can't wait to get a little older. My daddy
says that if other people help me, someday I might learn
how to snow ski, swim, play basketball and baseball
or even ride horses. I can't wait!

N is for Needing lots of help.
Right now, I need help to take a bath, get dressed,
go to the bathroom, and get in and out of the car.
I even need help to roll over in bed. Mommy says that
if I keep trying, I will need less and less help.
I'm trying hard, Mommy!

O is for Orthotics.
Mommy and Daddy call them braces. I have to wear
orthotics on my feet to help me stand. They help my feet
and ankles become straight and strong. I stand better
when I wear them. I also have braces for my hands
that help me hold things and play.

P is for Power Wheelchair.
One day I might be strong enough to drive a power wheelchair. It has a joystick to push to make it go. I am trying to learn now. I love to go fast, but I keep going in circles and circles. I have some work to do.

Q is for Quadriplegia.

That is a big word that means both my arms and my legs are stiff. I have quadriplegia. Some people with cerebral palsy only have stiff legs. They have diplegia. Some people with cerebral palsy just have one side of their body stiff. That is hemiplegia.

R is for Ramps.
Ramps help me go in and out of my house and van.
There is a ramp to go to my school, to the store, and
to the restaurants where we eat. I love ramps.
Ramps make steps so much easier.

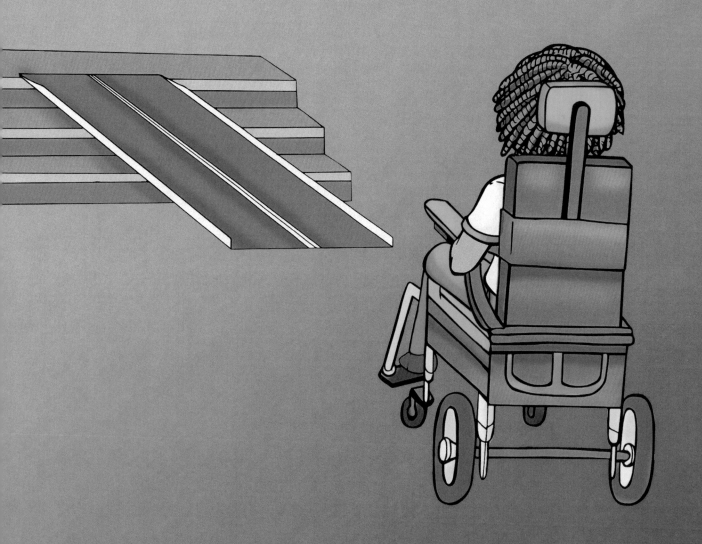

S is for Seizures.

Seizures are kind of like when your computer or TV screen messes up for a little bit. Electricity runs a computer. A different kind of electricity runs everyone's brain. When the electricity in my brain gets jumbled, I have a seizure. I might stare off into space. I might jerk, or I might shake. Usually my seizures last less than a minute.

T is for Talking.
I talk slowly. I don't always say my words like you do.
Mommy and Daddy understand me when I tell them
what I want, but other people have trouble. So,
sometimes I use a special computer to help me talk.

U is for Understanding.
People talk about me right in front of my face!
Talk to me please! My ears work fine, and
I understand what you are saying!

V is for our Awesome Van.
Our van takes me places with my family.
It has a ramp for my wheelchair.
This weekend we went to the beach.
I love the beach!

W is for Wonder.
I wonder why people stare at me when they first meet me. I wonder why people ask what's wrong with me…when there is so much right with me. I wonder if one day you'll forget about my wheelchair and just see how fun I am.

X is for Excited.
I am so excited that you know about cerebral palsy now.
Maybe now you and I can be friends.

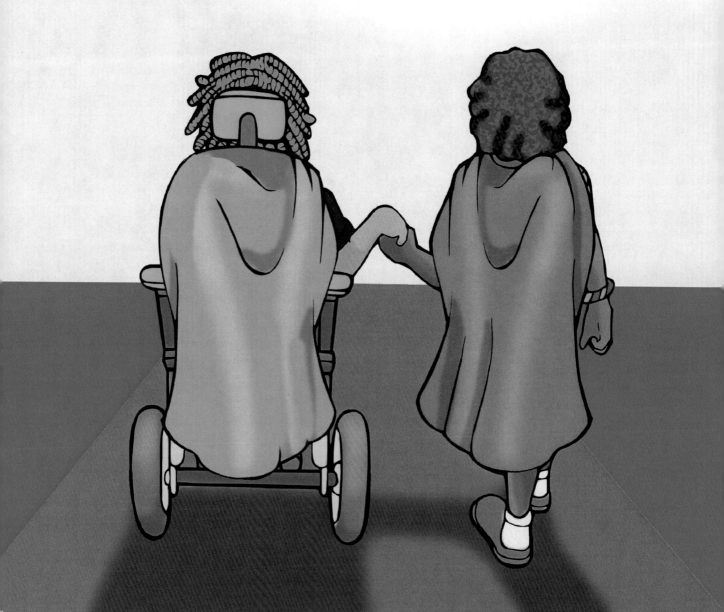

Y is for Yes.
You and I can be great friends! Can you take me
for a stroll in my wheelchair? I love to feel the
wind in my hair and the bump, bump, bumps
under my wheels.

Z is for Zoom!
Zip over here, and let's go!
Zoooooooom!

The end.

Consider these 3 requests from a child
with cerebral palsy:

◇◇

3-Step Action Plan
1. Include Me
2. Encourage Me
3. Expect Great Things from Me

Other offerings by the author:

◇◇

Books:
A is for Autism

D is for Down Syndrome

YouTube Channel:
Pediatric Physical Therapy Exercises

Facebook page:
Pediatric Physical Therapy Exercises

Instagram:
PediatricPTExercises

Pinterest:
amysturkey/pediatric-physical-therapy

About the Illustrator

Ikos Ronzkie is an international graphic designer, book illustrator, and comic strip artist. She creates fanciful illustrations for advertisements, campaigns, comic books, character designs, book designs and book covers. She has worked as an illustrator with local and international clientele for over 15 years.

She illustrated this author's previous 2 books *A is for Autism* and *D is for Down Syndrome*. She is also the illustrator for books including: *What Babies Do, Oh, Livvie!, What Do I Do Well, The Loosey Goosey Tooth, Princess Superhero Antonia, The Tooth Fairy, My Daddy's Hat* and *Willie Nilly Adventures*.

Her clients include international publishers, dollmakers, comic book writers, authors, and picture book writers. She produces *"Bayan ng Biyahero Comics"* for the Antipolo Star Newspaper for the Rizal and Metro Manila distribution areas. She previously created *"Estudyante Blues"* for the Living News and Good Education magazine. Independently, she writes and produces her own comics: *"Karit," "Dalawang Liham," "Sulsi,"* and the webcomics, *"Hilda Intrimitida."*

Ronzkie is the co-founder of IKOS Komiks which strives to promote and explore Philippine culture with visual and literary arts. Their creations are dedicated to work inspired by the Philippine history, myths and legends.

◇◇◇◇◇◇◇◇◇◇◇◇◇◇◇◇◇◇◇◇◇◇◇◇◇◇◇◇

Made in United States
North Haven, CT
26 February 2023

33222204R00022